Christmas
COLOR BY NUMBERS

Christmas
COLOR BY NUMBERS

Georgie Fearns

SIRIUS

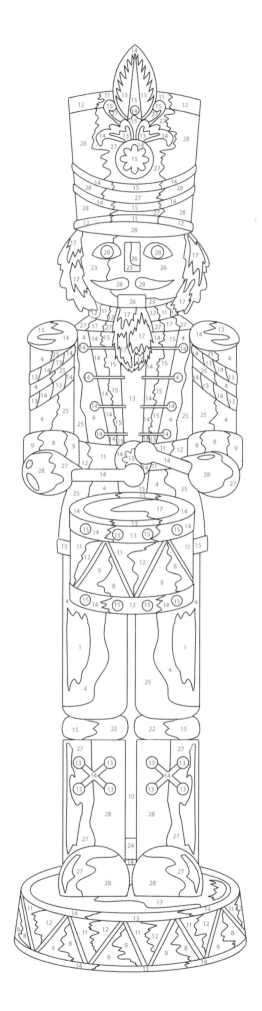

SIRIUS

This edition published in 2023 by Sirius Publishing, a division of
Arcturus Publishing Limited,
26/27 Bickels Yard, 151–153 Bermondsey Street,
London SE1 3HA

Copyright © Arcturus Holdings Limited

ISBN: 978-1-3988-2063-0
CH010156NT
Supplier 29, Date 0423, PI 00004736

Printed in China

Introduction

It's a time for remembering the true story of Christmas, for family gatherings and for celebrating a wealth of traditions that have accrued over the centuries. In this joyous color-by-numbers book, artist Georgie Fearns has put together a delightful selection of images inspired by Christmas.

You'll find Santa and his sleigh traveling over the rooftops, stockings packed with treats, marshmallows toasting over a crackling fire, and Christmas wreaths adorning a front door surrounded by snow. There are snow globes, holly trees bursting with berries, skaters on a frozen pond, and a Christmas pudding waiting for everyone to dig in. A ski lodge sits, its windows glowing in a snowy night, children sledge down a hill thick with fresh-laid snow, and an angel trumpets the glad tidings of a new Christmas morning. It's a heartwarming collection that evokes all aspects of Christmas.

Coloring-by-numbers is a great way to gain confidence in art. Each image is numbered using the key given on the back flap of this book. All you need to do is follow the color key and you'll soon build up to a professional-looking colored drawing—your own celebration of a special time.

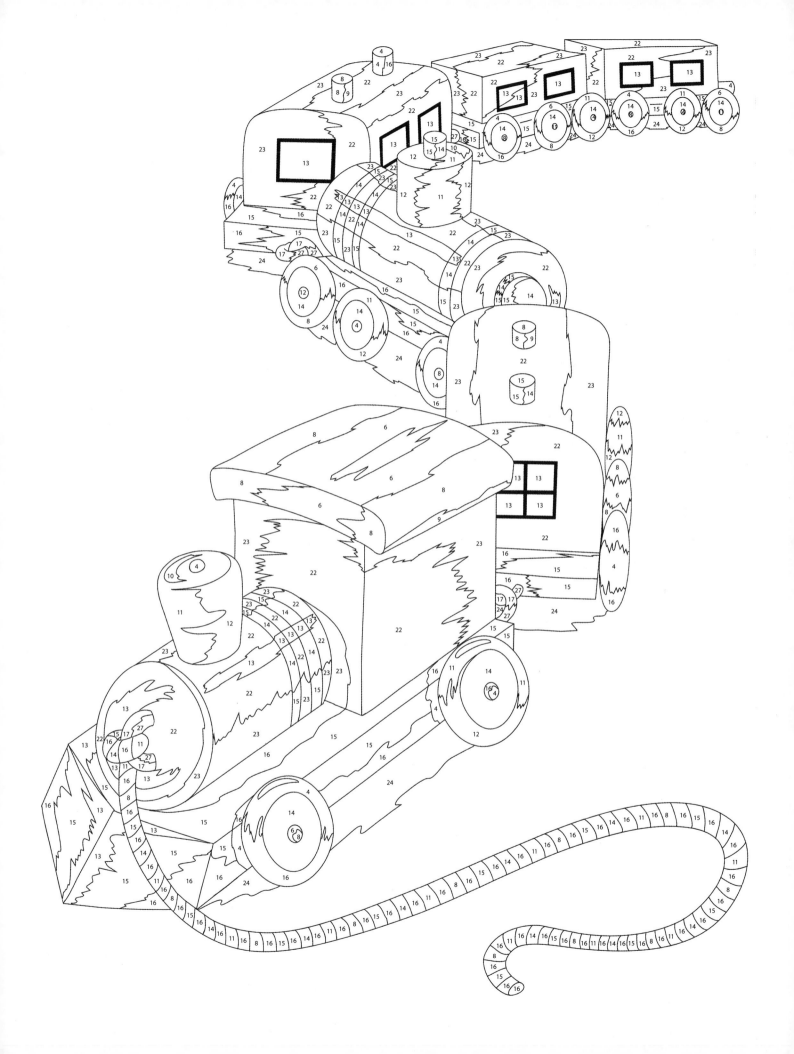

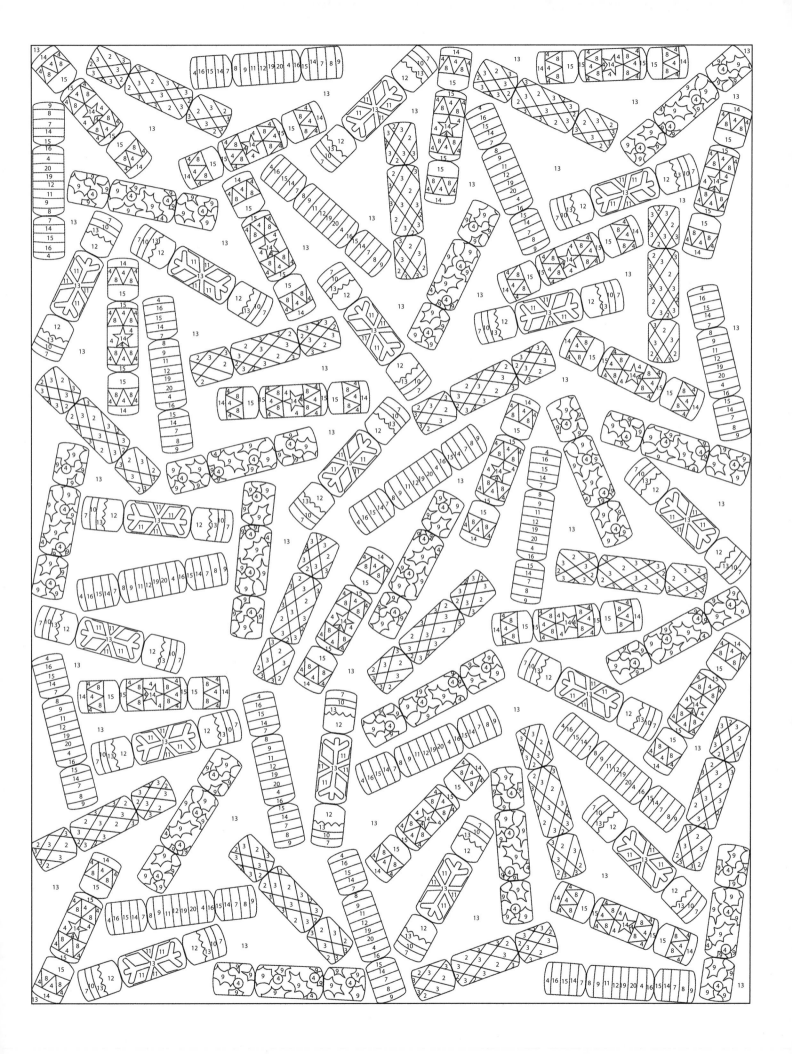

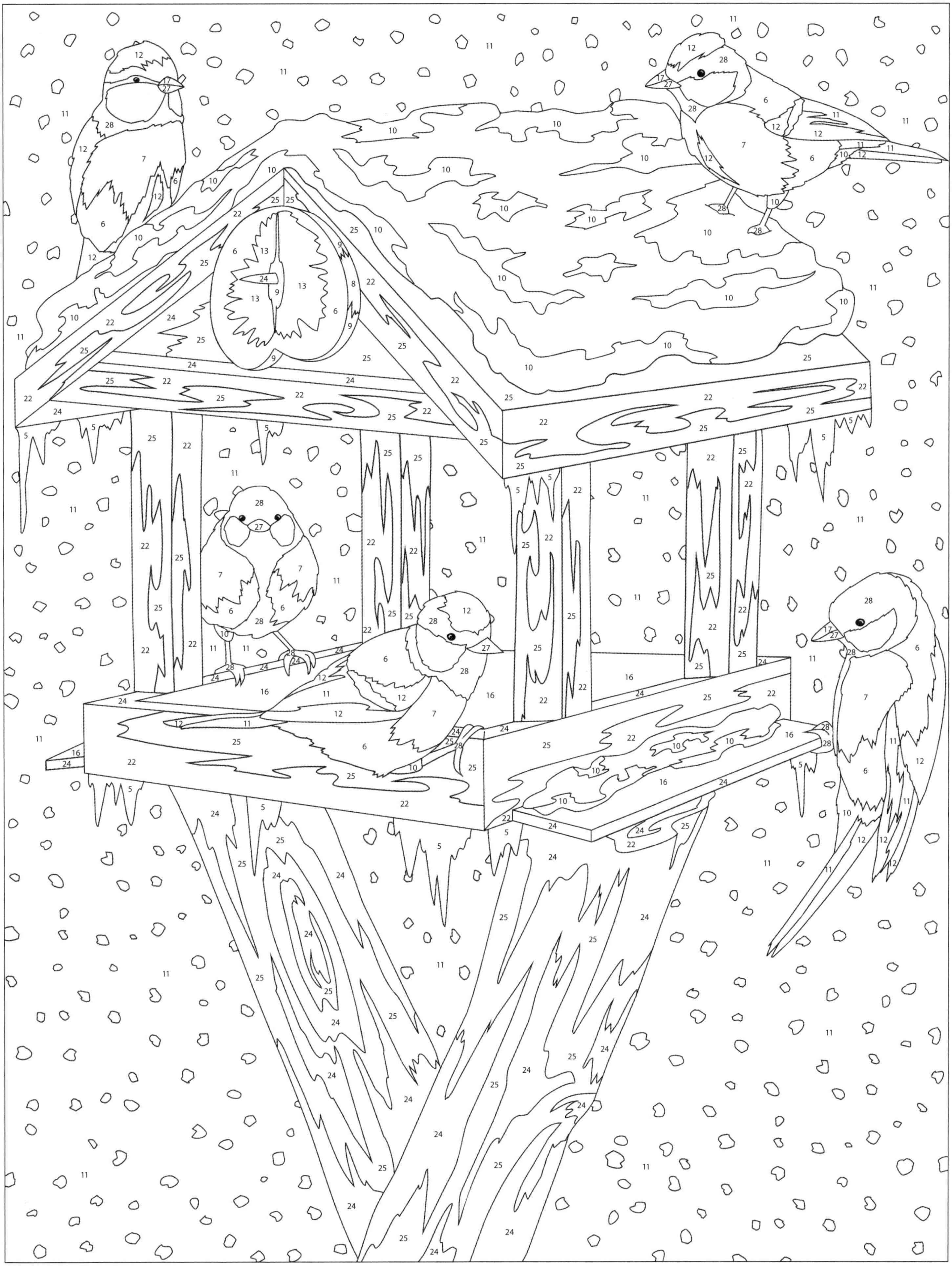